WORLD SOCCER CLUBS

AC MILAN

by Derek Moon

Copyright © 2025 by Press Room Editions. All rights reserved. No part of this book may be used or reproduced in any manner whatsoever, including internet usage, without written permission from the copyright owner, except in the case of brief quotations embodied in critical articles and reviews.

Book design by Kate Liestman
Cover design by Kate Liestman

Photographs ©: Jonathan Moscrop/Sportimage/Cal Sport Media/AP Images, cover; Jonathan Moscrop/Getty Images Sport/Getty Images, 5, 7; Chris Ricco/Getty Images Sport/Getty Images, 9; Shutterstock Images, 11; Carlo Fumagalli/AP Images, 13; Alessandro Sabattini/Getty Images Sport/Getty Images, 15, 17, 19; Ben Radford/Allsport/Getty Images Sport/Getty Images, 21; Etsuo Hara/Getty Images Sport/Getty Images, 23, 27; Giuseppe Bellini/Getty Images Sport/Getty Images, 25; Clive Rose/Getty Images Sport/Getty Images, 28

Press Box Books, an imprint of Press Room Editions.

ISBN
978-1-63494-955-2 (library bound)
978-1-63494-969-9 (paperback)
979-8-89469-000-1 (epub)
978-1-63494-983-5 (hosted ebook)

Library of Congress Control Number: 2024940745

Distributed by North Star Editions, Inc.
2297 Waters Drive
Mendota Heights, MN 55120
www.northstareditions.com

Printed in the United States of America
012025

ABOUT THE AUTHOR

Derek Moon is an author who lives in Watertown, Massachusetts, with his wife and daughter.

TABLE OF CONTENTS

CHAPTER 1
CHAMPIONS OF ITALY 4

CHAPTER 2
RISE OF MILAN..........10

CHAPTER 3
EUROPE'S FINEST 16

SUPERSTAR PROFILE
PAOLO MALDINI 22

CHAPTER 4
A NEW ERA............ 24

QUICK STATS 30
GLOSSARY 31
TO LEARN MORE 32
INDEX..........32

CHAPTER 1

CHAMPIONS OF ITALY

Zlatan Ibrahimović was bold. The striker scored goals most players wouldn't even try. But when he first arrived at AC Milan in January 2020, expectations were low. Milan is one of Europe's most storied clubs. However, the team had fallen below its standards. The *Rossoneri* (Red and Blacks) had not won Italy's top league, Serie A,

Zlatan Ibrahimović often tried to score in acrobatic ways.

since 2011. Milan sat in 11th place when Ibrahimović arrived. At 38 years old, he wanted to see if he could still thrive at the top level.

"Ibra" proved he still had it. The giant Swede scored 10 goals in 18 games. He also added five assists. By season's end, Milan had moved up to sixth place. The next year, Ibrahimović scored a team-high

THE LAST SCUDETTO

Zlatan Ibrahimović had a previous stint with AC Milan. In 2011, he helped the club win its 18th *scudetto*. That's the nickname for a Serie A championship. Ibrahimović scored 14 goals that season. No one on the team scored more. A year later, he led the team with 28. However, he left the team after that season.

Rafael Leão (17) recorded 14 goals and 12 assists for AC Milan during the 2021–22 season.

15 goals. He helped Milan finish in second place. The team hadn't finished that high since 2012.

The Rossoneri had rallied around Ibrahimović. But they still hadn't achieved their main goal. AC Milan's biggest rival,

7

Inter Milan, had won the title in 2021. In 2022, the title race turned into a battle of the Milan clubs. On the last day of the season, AC Milan played at Sassuolo. A win or tie would secure the title for the Rossoneri. Thousands of fans made the trip from Milan.

Winger Rafael Leão had been a breakout star that season. In the 17th minute, he raced up the left wing. Then he cut inside. He rolled a pass to Olivier Giroud. The veteran forward sent the ball into the net for a 1–0 lead. Later in the first half, Leão set up Giroud for a second goal. And four minutes after that, midfielder Franck Kessié scored. Leão once again earned the assist.

AC Milan players celebrate after winning the Serie A title in 2022.

The drama was over. Milan fans rejoiced. The Rossoneri had finally claimed their 19th Serie A title. This was their first in 11 years. Ibrahimović called it the most satisfying title in his long career.

CHAPTER 2

RISE OF MILAN

Late in 1899, a group of Englishmen got together. They were living in the northern Italian city of Milan. They missed the sports from home. So, that December, they created a new soccer and cricket club. The founders gave Milan its red and black colors.

The team experienced many changes in the early years. The biggest came

With a metro population of more than three million people, Milan is the second-largest city in Italy.

in 1908. That year, some members wanted the club to sign more foreign players. Those members left to create Internazionale. That club is now known as Inter Milan. Meanwhile, Milan went by different names. In 1939, it became "Associazione Calcio Milan." That means Soccer Association Milan.

Milan enjoyed some early success. But then it went more than 40 years without a league title. The team looked abroad to change that. In 1948, Sweden won the Olympic gold medal in soccer. Forwards Gunnar Gren, Gunnar Nordahl, and Nils Liedholm led the way. The trio, known as Gre-No-Li, joined Milan shortly after the Olympics. Their goals led the Rossoneri

Gunnar Gren (left), Gunnar Nordahl (center), and Nils Liedholm (right) scored a combined 56 goals during the 1950–51 season.

to the Serie A title in 1951. Nordahl went on to score a record 221 career goals for Milan. He also led Serie A in scoring a record five times.

Liedholm stayed at Milan the longest. He helped Milan reach the 1958 European

Cup final. The tournament had been founded two years earlier. These days, it's known as the Champions League.

Gianni Rivera drove Milan to even greater heights. The creative midfielder was 17 when he joined the club in 1960. He earned the nickname "Golden Boy."

DERBY DELLA MADONNINA

AC Milan was once known as the city's working-class team. Today, Milan and Inter enjoy support all over the world. But they remain fierce rivals. The neighbors have shared the San Siro stadium since 1947. They've also been highly successful. As a result, their matches are often important. When the teams play, the game is called the *Derby della Madonnina*. The Madonnina is a famous statue in Milan.

In 1969, Gianni Rivera (left) became the first Italian-born player to win the Ballon d'Or. At the time, that trophy was given to the best player in Europe.

Rivera went on to appear in 658 matches. Milan won every major trophy during this period. That included the 1963 European Cup. Milan became the first Italian team to win it. Then Milan won the tournament again in 1969.

CHAPTER 3

EUROPE'S FINEST

Gianni Rivera played his final game in 1979. He left Milan with a scudetto. But dark times were coming. An illegal betting scheme spread in Italian soccer. Milan was involved. And the team got punished for it. Milan was sent to Italy's second division, Serie B.

Milan played its way back into Serie A quickly. But the team had lost

Marco van Basten scored 90 goals in 147 Serie A games for AC Milan.

money playing in Serie B. By 1986, funds were running out. A new owner stepped in to save the team. Silvio Berlusconi grew up a Milan fan. Then he made a fortune in TV and other business. He used a lot of that money to revive the club.

The team already had some talented players. Captain Franco Baresi anchored the defense. Teenage left back Paolo Maldini looked promising. But Berlusconi wanted more stars. Milan brought in Ruud Gullit and Marco van Basten before the 1987–88 season. The Dutch stars led Milan back to the top of Serie A. Then Dutch midfielder Frank Rijkaard joined the next season. With that core, Milan became a force.

AC Milan players celebrate after winning the 1989 European Cup.

A talented Real Madrid team awaited in the semifinal of the 1989 European Cup. Milan dismantled the Spanish team 5–0. Then the Rossoneri won the final with ease. Gullit and Van Basten scored two goals each. One year later, Milan repeated as European champs. Rijkaard scored the lone goal in the final.

Fabio Capello had coached Milan's youth teams in the 1980s. In 1991, he took over as manager of the senior team. And he kept the Rossoneri humming. They went 58 games without a loss. Milan won three straight Serie A titles. The club reached three straight Champions League finals, too.

A NEW WAY TO PLAY

Manager Arrigo Sacchi arrived at Milan in 1987. Most fans hadn't heard of the Italian. Soon, his new tactics changed the game. At the time, most Italian teams focused on defense and counterattacks. But Sacchi's teams played an organized, high-pressing style. Every player was involved. In 1991, Sacchi left to coach the Italian men's national team.

Franco Baresi (left) played his entire career for AC Milan.

Behind Baresi and Maldini, Milan played suffocating defense in 1994. But scoring goals was a challenge. That changed in the Champions League final. Milan dominated Barcelona in a 4–0 victory. The Rossoneri couldn't be stopped.

SUPERSTAR PROFILE

PAOLO MALDINI

Defender Cesare Maldini joined AC Milan in 1954. As team captain, he led Milan to its first European title in 1963. Maldini retired as a club legend. Then he helped the team even after he stopped playing.

Cesare's son Paolo Maldini joined Milan's youth ranks at age 10. He made his debut with the senior team at 16. For the next 25 years, Milan was set at left back. Paolo Maldini's pure defensive skills were unmatched. So was his leadership. Maldini served as Milan's captain for more than a decade.

Maldini retired from Italy's national team in 2002. He stayed with Milan until 2009. Maldini played more than 900 games for the Rossoneri. His teams won five European titles. They added seven scudettos. Many legends have played for Milan. But no one has brought home as many trophies as Maldini.

Paolo Maldini received only four red cards in his 25-year career.

CHAPTER 4

A NEW ERA

Fabio Capello left Milan in 1996. His teams had won four scudettos in five seasons. After two down seasons, Milan won the league again in 1999. Defense remained a strength. Veterans Paolo Maldini and Alessandro Costacurta weren't slowing down. And a new group of stars had arrived.

Andrea Pirlo transferred from Inter to AC Milan in 2001.

Striker Andriy Shevchenko joined Milan in 1999. He scored 48 league goals over the next two seasons. Keeper Dida, midfielder Andrea Pirlo, and forward Filippo Inzaghi soon joined him. Those players drove the team to the 2003 Champions League final. Milan faced off against Serie A rival Juventus. The game came down to a shootout. Shevchenko's clutch penalty kick secured Milan's sixth European title.

The Rossoneri reached Champions League finals again in 2005 and 2007. In 2005, they led 3–0 at halftime. However, Liverpool made a stunning comeback and won in a shootout. The same teams met again in 2007. Milan was still loaded with talent. Attacking midfielder Kaká

Filippo Inzaghi celebrates after scoring in the 2007 Champions League final.

was named the world's best player that season. And Inzaghi scored twice in the final. That lifted Milan to a 2–1 victory.

Milan continued to bring in big stars. Striker Zlatan Ibrahimović led the team to the 2011 scudetto. Trouble was coming, though. The team built up a lot of debt.

Theo Hernández (19) recorded five goals and six assists in Serie A during the 2021–22 season.

In 2017, new owners bought the team. But Milan's struggles continued.

Paolo Maldini finally turned Milan around. The club legend became technical director in 2019. Maldini brought in talented players such as Theo Hernández and Rafael Leão. He also hired Stefano Pioli as manager. Some fans didn't want the former Inter coach. Milan fans fully embraced him when the team won the scudetto in 2022. Milan was back to being one of Italy's best teams.

SAN SIRO

AC Milan moved into the San Siro in 1926. A century later, the Rossoneri still play there. With more than 75,000 seats, the San Siro is one of Europe's biggest stadiums. Many famous games have taken place there. Two of the most heated came in the 2023 Champions League semifinal. Inter and Milan faced off against each other. However, Inter defeated Milan in both games.

QUICK STATS

AC MILAN

Founded: 1899

Home stadium: San Siro

Serie A titles: 19

European Cup/Champions League titles: 7

Coppa Italia titles: 5

Key managers:

- Arrigo Sacchi (1987–91, 1996–97): 1 Serie A title, 2 European Cup titles
- Fabio Capello (1991–96, 1997–98): 4 Serie A titles, 1 Champions League title
- Carlo Ancelotti (2001–09): 1 Serie A title, 2 Champions League titles, 1 Coppa Italia title

Most career appearances: Paolo Maldini (902)

Most career goals: Gunnar Nordahl (221)

Stats are accurate through the 2023–24 season.

GLOSSARY

assists
Passes that lead directly to goals.

captain
A player who serves as the leader of a team.

clutch
A difficult situation when the outcome of the game is in question.

debt
Money that is owed.

debut
First appearance.

high-pressing
When a team loses possession of the ball and its forwards put a lot of pressure on the opposing defenders to stop them from advancing up the field.

rival
An opposing player or team that brings out the greatest emotion from fans and players.

shootout
A way of deciding a tie game. Players from each team take a series of penalty kicks.

veteran
A player who has spent several years in a league.

TO LEARN MORE

Hewson, Anthony K. *GOATs of Soccer*. North Mankato, MN: Abdo Publishing, 2022.

McDougall, Chrös. *The Best Rivalries of World Soccer*. Minneapolis: Abdo Publishing, 2024.

Snow, Kevin. *AC Milan*. New York: Cavendish Square, 2021.

MORE INFORMATION

To learn more about AC Milan, go to **pressboxbooks.com/AllAccess**. These links are routinely monitored and updated to provide the most current information available.

INDEX

Baresi, Franco, 18, 21

Capello, Fabio, 20, 24
Costacurta, Alessandro, 24

Dida, 26

Giroud, Olivier, 8
Gren, Gunnar, 12
Gullit, Ruud, 18–19

Hernández, Theo, 29

Ibrahimović, Zlatan, 4, 6–7, 9, 27
Inzaghi, Filippo, 26–27

Kaká, 26–27
Kessié, Franck, 8

Leão, Rafael, 8, 29
Liedholm, Nils, 12–13

Maldini, Paolo, 18, 21, 22, 24, 28

Nordahl, Gunnar, 12–13

Pioli, Stefano, 29
Pirlo, Andrea, 26

Rijkaard, Frank, 18–19
Rivera, Gianni, 14–15, 16

Shevchenko, Andriy, 26

van Basten, Marco, 18–19